# Ellipsis

# •••

## The Lockdown Poems

# Steve Wheeler

First published by
Wheelsong Books
4 Willow Close, Plymouth PL3 6EY,
United Kingdom

First published in 2020

Print ISBN 979-8-66641-525-2

For JC

# Contents

# Thank You

My grateful thanks go to my wife Dawn (my favourite teacher of English) for her unwavering love, support and honesty, and to my daughters Amy and Kate and my son Sam for their constant good humour, encouragement and occasional cups of tea (Earl Grey, white, no sugar).

When I succumbed to Covid, Dawn and Sam looked after me and helped me to recovery even though Dawn was unwell herself. My heroes.

I also thank my father Kenneth R. V. Wheeler for his 92 years of inspiration, verbal sparring and his many colourful reminiscences, all of which add fuel to the fire.

Finally, I thank my family, friends and colleagues everywhere, because most of the sales of this book will be probably be attributed to them.

Steve Wheeler
July 2020

# The Intermission

This new collection of poems and reflections was written, as the title suggests, during the lockdown. This verse represents various perspectives, some very personal, some a lot more general. Some are fictional, some related to my own experiences – you decide. The poetry is written in a variety of styles, often in keeping with the mood I was in at the time, but sometimes as a deliberate method to evoke images and thoughts about the experiences I and many, many others went through during the months at the height of the pandemic.

This has been traumatic, horrific, devastating, but also challenging, inspirational and at times, even a strangely joyful time. To reflect this, some of the poems are dark and some downright depressing or intensely introspective. Others are lighter and laced with my attempts at humour.

No-one was prepared for the Coronavirus pandemic. The crisis caused worldwide panic, and the horrors that followed could easily have been taken from the script of an apocalyptic movie. The lights suddenly went out in our society. Airports, train stations and even the roads outside our homes fell strangely silent, while our hospitals and clinics became hives of furious, life-or-death activity.

Our lives were paused. We were in an intermission and no-one knew just how long it might last. In the midst of our uncertainty, we learned to cherish the things we hold most dear. Our loved ones, our health, our security, our lives. We also got used to the regular washing of hands, wearing masks and perversely, steering clear of strangers and friends alike.

I named this selection of poems *Ellipsis* for a very good reason. English scholars will tell you that an ellipsis can be found in texts as a series of three dots … used by authors to signify an omission that does not alter the meaning of the text.

In the same way, although we have all suffered an omission in our lives – some the loss of a loved one, others the loss of their income or employment, still others a long term damage to their health – we have not lost the meaning of our existence, nor have we lost hope – hope for change, hope for doing things better, hope for a better life.

This was witnessed in the *Black Lives Matter* movement which challenged everyone's thinking about how we should treat each other. It was seen in the heroism and resilience of elderly people raising money for charity, or in celebrities using their fame to speak out for the good of society.

The drastic and sudden interruption in travel resulted in huge falls in carbon emissions across the globe. Traffic on the roads was almost zero at the height of the pandemic, and it was an eerie experience to walk out and hear no engine noises.

Rivers and skies became clearer, and nature slowly began to recover a little from decades of human onslaught. Families were separated for a very long period during lockdown where only technology could keep people in touch with their loved ones.

This would not have been possible even a few years ago, but now everyone was learning to communicate over a distance as they were forced to work from home.

These situations gave many of us cause to reconsider our relationships and value those we care about more.
It made some of us wonder why we would travel to work for an hour or more each day on a cramped, overheated, dirty transport system such as a train or tube.

We began to appreciate the little things in life that we had previously taken for granted. This was our ellipsis – an enforced omission of activity in our lives that was illustrated with harrowing, heart-breaking stories but also tempered with heroism, hope and a determination to make our world a better place.

We would be foolish if, after all we have endured, we lost sight of this meaning. We will waste this opportunity, born out of a global threat, if we go back to being just the same as we were before.

It's interesting what you can see when the lights have been turned off.

Steve Wheeler
Plymouth, July 2020

# Breaking News

tv media papers website clicks
underhanded surreptitious pics
paparazzi allegation sticks
police protest riots flying bricks

photo flashing blue lights tragic news
propaganda banners racist views
dangerous streets children without shoes
city winners win and losers lose

vandals demonstrations tear gas clouds
job loss protest marches mindless crowds
corona epidemic storm-clouds
carnage piled-up bodies burial shrouds

police brutal justice in the mire
thoughtless arson 5G towers on fire
looting violence presidential liar
nations writhing on a funeral pyre

conspiracy theories believe the fake
lurid headlines stories made to break
fearful thinking mental trauma quake
breaking broadcast news for news' sake

# 2020 Vision

January – Brexit anxiety
February – Flood damage / broken society
March – Covid 19 / abject fear
April – Pandemic deaths a curse
May – More of the same and worse
June – Who knows where we go from here?

Half the year is over now
Take a breath / mop the brow
We can't undo what has been done.
Can we please fast forward to 2021?

# Lockdown Blues

I'm caught in a limbo
with much to decide
Do I write me a poem
or take a walk outside?

Do I binge watch some box sets
on the Beeb or Netflix
Raid my CD collection
for a musical fix?

Do I sit and compose
on my keyboard or guitar?
Find a good book to read
or drive off in my car?

Do I Skype an old friend
and for hours reminisce?
or something more pressing
and go take a .... toilet break

Should I stay in my house
or take leave of this place?
Will my choice be a triumph
or end in disgrace?

It's perfectly obvious
what I'm doing right now:
Staying home to make furrows
with a hand held plough

# I've never washed my hands so much

I've never washed my hands so much
and every surface that I touch
is disinfected regular, like
so to avoid a second spike.

My fingernails and hair have grown
to lengths that previously were unknown.
The endless wear of casual clothes
has only added to my woes.

I cannot visit elderly aunts
and still maintain correct distance,
insisting as they do on hugs
and kisses that might pass on bugs.

Now shopping is a dangerous game
with supermarket one way lanes
and queues that snake both ways outside
for hours and hours 'til once inside,
the shelves are empty of essentials
'cos panic buyers chucked a mental.

If only they would use their brains,
they'd stop this nonsense and refrain
The toilet paper, soap and Cif
grow in mountains where they live.

This surplus is a sight obscene
and shows how stupid folks have been.

# Fascinated by clouds

I'm fascinated by the clouds
Their ever changing shapes and hues
The way they reflect the light
While merging into the blue

I'm fascinated by the clouds and
The pictures in their vapour I can find
Recognisable images of familiar things
That play reflections in my mind

Moving, going
Fleeting, showing
Never knowing
Forever flowing

I'm fascinated by the clouds
Creeping slowly across my vision in array
The slowly boiling movement flows
To take me captive as they fly away

It's better far to be looking up than down at our situation
It's more efficacious
in this time of crisis in our nation
To gaze upon the subtle
movement high above us
Than to focus on
the creeping enemy that assails us

# WFH

In my living room
I've made space for Zoom
and various paraphernalia

I'll be regularly Skyping,
and e-mail typing
and a dozen other ways
to hail ya

We'll keep in touch
for work and such-like
ways to earn a few quid

But please don't rely
on an immediate reply
'cos I'm working from home
with three kids

# In Limbo

Another day spent in this limbo
One more from off the calendar is marked
The hours tick by, the four walls closing in
The minutes of my mind decreasing in their arc

There is no ending to this torrid journey
No resolution to this harrowing distress
No final hurdle yet appears on the horizon
And still the hours continue to progress

Another day decays in silent limbo
The same routine, no deviation or respite
There is no variation to this turgid theme
The minutes and the hours bleed into night

# White Noise

I was up at five again today to see the summer light stream
through the curtain but it wasn't this that brushed my torrid
dreams aside it was more likely the turbulence of life in fact
I'm certain

that since the crisis hit us like a slow burning conflagration my
brain has been exercised by thoughts of creeping doom and it
doesn't take too much imagination for my tired suggestible
mind to irrationally assume

that everyone I hold most dear must surely succumb and I
will be the bearer of a lethal infection. But this although a
remote possibility is pretty dumb to dwell upon when it robs
me of my sleep and is only a vivid confection

of a strained imagination. My dreaming offers little respite
contorted as it is in strange contrived and convoluted tropes
and it makes me feel as though each night my rest is disturbed
and rearranged as I am led away in ropes

of anxiety down dark highways of doubt and fear to places
surreal and disturbing to a rational mind and every night the
visions rear in mists of imaginings that are at once palpably
unreal yet if I allow them to be so perturbing.

I was up at five again today to watch the dawn break silently
beyond my window pane and I am so very tired of all the
white noise in my life and how it tries to shake my soul but in
the final analysis another day of this has started

and I am simply weary once again.

# Sleeping Alone

The words go rushing
and backtracking
lyrics lost inside a palindrome

Forever my mind
is choking with the
freeform and nonsensical phrases
that aimlessly roam
progressing relentlessly
through the restless
themes of yesterday
and the misdemeanours
of the night
that plague my
every waking day

I yearn for solace
like a wounded dog in open space
but the time comes crashing
down around me
while indifferent walls
stare blindly
and the ticking behind
the clock face
reminds me
there can be no returning

Isolation screams silently
and regret floods
inundating inwardly
like some thoughtless
act of sabotage
a vandalism of the soul

This sordid awakening
that often overwhelms
but never satisfies
or makes whole

This cheap and vapid perfume
that wrecks and
ruins and dissipates

The switch has been thrown
and I sleep alone

# Zoom, He Went

Zoom, he went,
'cos Zoom was all he had,
to span the distance
stretching out in all directions
to bridge the chasms made
by enemies so small
that none would ever see them
but all would know and rue
the path of devastation that they laid.

Zoom he went,
and zooming into ether
his visage was quickly sent,
full motion, to those rooms
and halls and spaces
of all those who complied
that were embellished
by the ghostly presence
in case the social died.

Zoom he went,
and zoom became his reach
fast flowing, connecting him
to others who were similarly bent
on being with the ones they loved
even though there was no touch
no close proximity to hands
and all the love they sent.

Zoom he went,
and zoom he did
and zoomed he was
but his images were frozen,
the signal lost and fell.

His voice became distorted
his image pixelated
and contact was disrupted
and never reconnected
but he was never moved.

So Zoom became his prison cell.

# That first Thursday

That first Thursday
I emerged from my front door
at eight pm
and stood in bare feet
on my doorstep
offering up my applause
my thanks
to unseen heroes
who somewhere were
battling an invisible enemy.

That first Thursday
I stood alone
in the safety of
my doorway in the
suburban close
where few could see
or hear my clapping.

And yet emotion
hit me like a wave
and my head dropped
and my vision blurred
as I thought of all those

who stared fear directly in the face
and confronted danger
without hesitation

to care for perfect strangers
they might never meet again.

My applause was
not enough.

But it was a start.

# Taking Stock

Welcome to our superstore
There's everything you'll ever need and more
Essential items are on display
such as all the ingredients for Pancake Day
We'll sell you lemons, sugar, eggs
but be aware we're running out of flour bags
We've sandwiches and ornate bowls
Alas, there are no toilet rolls

There's Easter eggs and potted plants
and frozen peas and underpants
and barbecues and packs of beer,
(Remember summer's almost here)
There's ready meals to sink a ship
Buy one get one free, but be quick
There's cod and hake and Dover sole,
but we're completely out of toilet roll

We do though, stock the Daily Mail
and other tabloids are on sale
and you can purchase all you need
From vegetables to packs of seed
There's a hundred different kinds of bread
or you could try our cakes instead
But some things are beyond our control
for instance, there's no toilet roll

Our goods are neatly piled in stacks
Select your items from the racks

Our special offers wait for you
from kitchenware to ladies' shoes
Slashing prices you can't ignore
Your trolley full, no room for more
But the panic buyers took their toll
We're sorry, there's no toilet roll

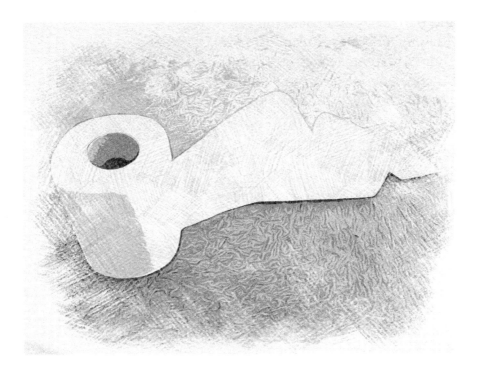

# Twice the Hero

Old man
Centenarian
Marching to victory
For a second time

His steps this
time less steady
but just as steadfast
as the first time
he strode forth
to serve his country

Old man
determined man
in a time of
global crisis
pushing body
to its limits

His resolve
no less diminished
with the passing of the years
as he recalls his service
and the duty
he fulfilled

Old man
Selfless man

Thinking not for himself
But always for others

Makes us admire
Makes others aspire
Makes him
twice the hero

# Forgetting for now

One day soon there will be an inquest they say
In the meantime, we are told to forget
    forget it for now, they say,
    we need to move on

Forgetting for now all the hope that we're needing
Forgetting for now all our cries and our pleading
Forgetting for now all the lies they're still feeding
Forgetting for now all the fears that are seeding
Forgetting the warnings we just were not heeding
Forgetting the stories of heartbreak we're reading

    and the politicians
    who are recklessly leading
    us all to the place
    where we're lost and we're bleeding

We may be told it's all worth forgetting
And we need to move on

    without any regretting
    but none of us can.
None of us could and
    none of us will

We have all lost so much
    but one thing we will never lose
    will be the memories

That is why we will never forget

# No Logic

A friend died today

There is no logic
and no comfort
when someone
you care for
simply
fades
away

# White Supremacy

Running through the city streets
marching to the Nazi beat
fists flailing, kicking feet
banners flying in the heat
of white supremacy

Every slogan that they shout
every slur that tumbles out
leaves us all in little doubt
their way of life is laced throughout
with white supremacy

See the mobs intent on killing
inward looking, lager swilling
in horror watch as blood is spilling
urban communities down-hilling
through white supremacy

It needs no great intelligence
to see that we should take offence
as the actions of the malcontents
cause mental scars of violence
through white supremacy

The readers of the Daily Mail
with tongues that wag and words that flail
the hatred rising off the scale
should tell us all from what we ail:
it's white supremacy

# Fear of difference

Fear of difference fear of other
though the black man is my brother
we're not the same as one another
still Black Lives Matter

Bigots of an elitist tribe
ethnicity and race divide
don't know don't care what beats inside
but Black Lives Matter

Indifference to those who've died
reveals your prejudice and pride
your diseased imagination lied
yet Black Lives Matter

Within the invective that you spew
you say that White Lives Matter too
but that's such an ignorant point of view
when Black Lives Matter

In the recesses of your mind
you seek no evidence to find
a reason to be colour blind
but Black Lives Matter

# Falling Structures

Inside the urban labyrinth
I came across an empty plinth
a place once occupied, that now
was empty, and I wondered how
a statue of such strong construction
could suffer great humiliation?

How what was once so safe and sound
could end up crashing to the ground,
its fractured pieces scattered far
and wide across the blackened tar.

The symbol of a darker time
was lying in the road supine,
no longer able to demand
attention, reverence or command.

And then a voice spoke in my ear
"This statue represented fear;
of bondage and a great oppression."
So I asked, in deep depression,
why would such structures be erected
so evil could be so prominently represented?

The answer came as I looked down
and saw the shoe marks all around,
that were not black, nor brown, nor white
but neutral prints, and then I saw the light:

When hatred speaks and you and I
ignore the threat and turn blind eyes,
symbols of hate and oppression thrive
to become the strong structures
that dominate our lives.

● ● ●

# No more plastic

Plastic, plastic, plastic
It's ubiquitously drastic
'Cos it ain't all that fantastic
Not plastic, no not plastic
I'm talking about plastic
Gets into everything quick
And you don't got to be scholastic
Or play no mental gymnastic
To see it's polluting the Atlantic
The Pacific and the Adriatic
And all the water you can stick
Making the oceans sick
Poisoning the public
Incredibly bombastic
It's plastic, that's plastic
It's totally nastric
It's disastric
I'm talking about plastic
It's a con-trick
On earth it's a cancer - neoplastic
Its flow is pyroclastic
Try to throw it away
and it comes back 'cos it's elastic
And I don't mean to sound sarcastic
But if you don't get this then,
yo man, u astic
It's statistically stochastic
That the world should not have plastic

It ain't iconoclastic
I'm talking about plastic
So don't manufacture no more plastic
We don't want no more plastic
We don't need no more plastic
And those that do
they need their ass kicked
We can't take no more plastic
'Cos it ain't all that fantastic
We need to do something drastic
To get rid of all that plastic
I'm talking about plastic
Can't take no more plastic

# Drying up

This is giving me a lot of consternation and I'm not sure if I
can give a coherent explanation 'cos the state I'm in right now
is a complication. It's not something I'm used to, not this
situation 'cos for the first time in my life I'm running out of
inspiration. I'm having to use some extra perspiration and a
deeper application.

Needing to put a little more effort in but it's hurting and I find
it kind of disconcerting
to think that my mind runs dry occasionally
and I'm not able to create so spontaneously
and I can't think of any new ideas to think
like my printer has just run out of its ink
and my keyboard is broken
and some of the letters don't work
and my Wi-Fi hub connection is going berserk
and my space bar is jammed and just keeps repeating and all
of my efforts are self-defeating
and my creativity is retreating
as my motivation is depleting
and I keep back spacing and deleting
and there's lots of white space that needs completing.

It's frightening to think that this might not be an intermission
and that drying up might become a permanent condition.
Just like in Grease the chills are multiplying
and I feel like I'm losing control

as my poetry is dying
and if I told you I was comfortable
with any of this
I would properly be lying
but I'm trying and I'm trying
and there ain't gonna be no denying
that any effort at all is better than nothing
and maybe even this attempt
at expressing myself
is something and whether I rap or I rhyme
or whether or not I can make it scan
I'm in need of a strategy
and I'm looking for a master plan
to keep my ideas going
to keep the poetry flowing
to keep the creativity showing
to stop the motivation slowing
it all boils down to this:

Get it down.
Get it down.

Get the verses onto the page and keep them going
round. Express myself in every way in lyrics
and in rhyme.

If I can do this I ain't gonna dry up
and I won't be wasting my time.

# Down

I am depressed
beyond
whatever I have
previously experienced
and I have
done this to myself
by obsessively watching
the news reports
caught up in the
harsh light from the TV set
watching in
horrid fascination
through my tears
as my world
destructs.

I am oppressed
beyond
what I can usually bear
as my mind
is crowded in
by scenes and statistics
that beggar belief
by lies and logistics
that will bring
no relief
by news that requires
more than
one handkerchief

there is nothing I can do
nowhere I can go
nothing I can give
to anyone

I am helpless
I am down,
and I am undone

# The virus and the damage done

As the vulnerable were
locked inside and shielded
then each of us in earnest
with our gods, we pleaded
to end the dread that raged
and roared about us
like a hurricane

Soon we began to slowly realise
that in our pain
none of us might ever
be the same again
for each of us our future
plans lost and conceded

As we watched each
yesterday accumulate
each day became yet
one more crossed off date
in a calendar of desolation
that stretched out before us
every one

The death count mounted
and infections spiralled on
not one of us could shield
our minds from the devastation

and the mental scarring
of the damage by the virus done

And now although we are not
without hope
within that miniscule
flickering of positivity
there lurks a certain
taint of inevitability
a sense that the damage
has already been done
and that no amount of
redemption can bring us
back out into the sun

And as the distance grows
around us and the innocence dies
the security that we once knew petrifies

And so as we emerge,
our eyes blinking with unease
into a brave new world
diminished by such insidious disease
we know that there will be
no more days in the sun
although each in our way
attempted to be shielded
our sanity was ultimately yielded
to the virus and the damage done

●　●　●

# The R

In case you really need to ask
although I have a homemade mask
I won't be going out at all
until the R rate starts to fall

Until the R rate falls to zero
I won't be acting like a hero
I will be strictly staying home
locked down inside my safety zone

To step outside my door would be
too dangerous for me, you see
some don't comply with health advice
their actions make the R rate rise

So replying to your RSVP
accept please, my apologies
I hope your birthday's second to none
and that your party will be fun
and you'll enjoy plenty of sun
but when everything is said and done
I'd rather stay at home, and be safe inside
than adding to the R rate rise

# Lockdown

The silence from the road below
is deafening because there are no
internal combustion engine sounds
all due to lockdown

The air above is fresh, and bird
song interrupts the spoken word
tranquillity is gaining ground
across the lockdown

No contrails in the crystal sky
pollutants no longer rising high
the atmosphere has settled down
during the lockdown

Clear air and water rushing by
to satisfy the jaundiced eye
I perversely wish for one more round
of the lockdown

# Weather Report

I'd rather not hear about the weather
Don't tell me about the storm
that's raging outside my door
I switched off all the weather reports long ago
I can't take the forecasts any more

Don't tell me about the isobars
the pressure lines that create the turbulence
the wind gusts and the sudden changes
the riotous rattling of the garden fence

The storm clouds that gather above
the fog of my mind and the mist in my soul
the winds that blew away our love
the time that you promised
you would make me whole

I don't want to know
how much rain is going to fall
how many tears would there be
if I counted them all
how many clouds are overhead
standing static,
brooding above me like lead

What I need to know is
when the sun bursts through
so I am standing in the light
in what alternative universe
will I ever get to have
a fair chance in this fight?

●　●　●

# Stick or Twist?

We're in the worst place
we can possibly be
caught between the virus
and the economy.
Do we stick or do we twist?
Either way it's a credible risk.

The government wants us to go out spending
but doesn't want this country to be trending
by rising up the mortality league list
and it's difficult to see
through the pandemic mist.

Should we stay safe in the lockdown
or open up the businesses in the town?
Though the transmission rates are coming down
we still have a virus named after a crown.

So while there's an active epidemic
and the infections are systemic
these questions are academic
because the outlook's not fantastic
and without meaning to sound bombastic
someone needs to get his ass kicked.

You see the politicians are in pieces
'cos they weren't prepared
for this kind of crisis,

---

but it's the common people
who are paying the price,
and no amount of apology
is going to suffice.

Our leaders had no training
for this amount of dying
but what they do possess
is a talent for lying
and while the entire world
is sat there crying
while all around us
our neighbours and families are dying
our so-called leaders
should be busy rectifying
all those initial mistakes that were made
all the misinformation
that was relayed
and the best laid plans
that were never laid
and the important decisions
that were delayed.

The question are still
unanswered as we
are caught between the virus
and the economy
and if we try to get back to

some sense of normality,
is how much carnage
are we going to see?

As the lockdown starts to ease
and everyone begins to do as they please
are we going to avoid
a wider spread of this disease,
catching the coughs
and stifling the sneeze?

Will we soon be worse off
than when we first began?
As we attempt to reboot our economic plan
will the social distancing rules be ignored?

Will we listen to the advice
from our overlords
or will it all be like
a monopoly board
… go back three spaces,
do not collect your reward?

Now no matter what the Government's stance is,
they're gonna throw their dice
and we'll all have to take our chances.

# Erasure

I have been told it's worth forgetting
for the sanity of the nation,
that we should think of better things
for our own self-preservation.

But is it worth omission
from our daily conversation,
so it's lost in the translation
and an alternative narration
from the top administration
prevents any 'complication'?

But for your information
there's a dawning realisation
of our leaders' limitations.

There was horrid fascination
as we saw the desolation
of the viral manifestation
in a global conflagration
through the mass contamination
of each and every civilisation.

And we heard the accusations
of the hurting generation
that endured the segregation,

Government procrastination
and the deadly hesitation,
and the media manipulation,
the bland interrogation,
and the truth assassination.

Horrific fascination
was the only punctuation
through our enforced isolation
with no hope of vaccination
or pandemic termination.

We heard endless proclamations
that brought wholesale confusion
and hopeless desperation
and the dire exasperation
of a fearful generation.

We saw betrayal of our nation
by the lies and humiliation
of political manipulation
with no fear of litigation
though the cries for resignation
led to bureaucratic violation
and power preservation.

Do not forget this.
Do not delete.
Erasure will not bring closure.

# YOLO

You only live once
so don't throw it away
don't act irresponsibly,
use common sense
keep acts of stupid abandon at bay
and maintain the correct social distance

You only live once,
so don't be a chump
by injecting yourself
with Domestos
if you listen to morons
like Donald Trump
you'll suffer a cardiac arrest-os

You only live once,
so don't hug or kiss
if you wish to survive this intact
wash your hands, wear a mask,
ignore those who diss
and avoid any physical contact

You only live once
so don't throw it away
don't act irresponsibly,
use common sense
keep acts of stupid abandon at bay
and maintain the correct social distance

# No Picnic

If you go down
to the woods today
you'll find that
they're not the same

The trees are gone
and the land is all bare
and you and me are to blame

'Cos everybody in the UK
is going down
for a Bic Mac today

Today's the day
we're swapping the forests
for beef steak

# Cadres

Noisy shouters,
Down and outers
Conspiracy theorists
Spreading fearists

Science doubters
Rule flouters
What abouters
Lager louters

Toothless cryers
Truthless liars
Snake oil buyers
Climate change deniers

Trolling sneerers
Haters, jeerers
Profiteerers
Selective hearers

News presenters
Crooked mentors
Life preventers
Confidence denters

Politicians
Statisticians
Bad musicians
Meteorological conditions

# Grades are grenades

Grades are grenades exploding in the mind like waves and wounding little children as they try to find a place to avoid the flying shrapnel of sarcasm and hide behind the walls they build and weep within a chasm of silence their faces contorted with confusion at the verbal violence.

Grades are like grenades

With remnants of regret they strive to avoid the bottom set while aspiring to be the teacher's pet which is something many grasp for but few will reach if the teacher is as cold as polar ice and does little more than teach and preach and throw content about like gambling dice.

Grades are like grenades

The curriculum is dour and should be rearranged but lesson plans pass through many hands unchanged, unrevised and undisturbed which leaves the children unprepared and much perturbed about where their future in society rests while expression and creativity matter less than tests.

Grades are like grenades

# History

These lines I've written down
may be only words to you
dark marks upon a
blank white page to you

To you they may be
little more than hieroglyphic
but let me take this from
the general to the specific
These meaningless scribbles
which to you might hold little value

I got to say that when you spoke them
words never failed you
unless I wrote them down
they really never came that easily to me
but these words express
what it's like for me to finally be
in a situation where I can
freely choose my destiny
so at the end of the day
girl you're history

And you may now be
throwing me some serious shade
but I hope you realise that
it was your behaviour that made
me write down these

feelings in the first place
and if I could I would for real
tell you this to your face

It was always unlike you
to give me any space
It was never in your neighbourhood
to show me any grace

Well now I'm gone girl
kick the dust right off my heels
You're history and I can't tell you
just how dope that feels

# Power is transitory

I'm not a glory seeker
but I am a fighter.
I've never been a novelist
but I am a writer,
and in all my days
and in all my ways
I've tried to be a straight-sighter
firing my literary bullets
into the dark to
try to make it lighter.

I'm a lyricist and whether in
a poem or in prose
I'm a line-by-line pugilist
and while the opposition runs and hides,
I will slug it out to document
the ugliness of society's great divides.

I'm a partisan and my conscience
tells me I'm a take sides,
because injustice is everywhere
and whatever the state provides
will never be enough
to heal humanity's wounded insides
and there's never gonna be any place to hide
because injustice and deprivation
always coincide.

Successive governments rise
and then they lose their popularity,
meet their demise

and fall, and they'll promise you
just about anything to persuade you
to heed their political call
but if they think
that's how the story ends
they're heading for a fall,
because the power of
the politician is transitory,
and nothing really changes.
No, it's something we can't ignore.

You see society is still
rotten through to the core
where the rich get richer
while the poor stay poor
and politicians must be judged
on whether they've made
any difference at all.

Politicians come to power
and they look for fame,
but how many of us
can remember any of their names,
'cos the bottom line is
no sooner than they screw it up
they resign and someone else comes in
and has to take the blame
and they do their
continuous damage
and none of them show any shame.

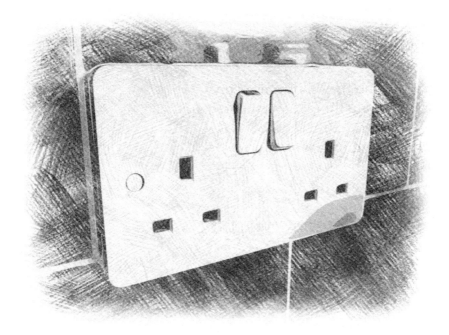

It's a constant rearrangement
and it's played out
like it was a board game.

No one who ever expresses
the remotest desire
to seize a position of power
should ever be allowed to
acquire authority over the people
'cos when it goes
down to the wire
they show no remorse
as they pursue their ideological desire
and none of them is willing
to pull us out from the fire.

The power we gain
in the here and now is transitory,
it passes in a flash
and that goes with the territory
because no matter how we try
to hold on to our personal glory
it slips right through
our grasping fingers with alacrity

and the next thing we know
we're standing right there in eternity
and it's only then
that we discover
with a stone cold certainty
that His is the only real power
and permanent glory.

And that's the real story.

Power is transitory.

• • •

# This is what grinds my gears

This is how to make my blood boil// this is what grinds my
gears// it's the thing that gives me constant cause for anger
and this is what reduces me to tears// it's a constant source of
trouble to me and something that can no longer be denied /
and it always bursts my bubble if I'm honest it's a painful
thorn in my side//
so feel it

Society is constantly subjected to the petty politics of power
and the consequence of this is inequality and this should be
the headline of the hour // but the fickle media jump from
one crisis to the other / and as soon as one goes out of vogue
we see them rushing
to another / it's not even hidden any more
it couldn't be more explicit that those in power
and the mass media are comfortably complicit//
take a break

We can always rely on the media to push us bad news more
obsessively than they should / as they seek out the tragic
headlines when they could be looking for the good but once a
story is no longer de rigueur/ they move quickly on to the
next news item and
that then becomes their *cri de cœur*//
so hear it

The public is its own worst enemy because the public
demands to be terrified / and the craving for a worst case
scenario needs to be satisfied// so their exploitative
journalistic methods can then be justified// as the media feed
on our compulsion to catastrophise// and misery is all we'll
ever know because it's right before eyes//
so see it

What hacks me off the most is the energy and resources the
press will spend to expose a celebrity's grief// or reporting on
the fall from grace of a popular football club chief// executive
while they ignore the inequality / and the deprivation in our
community / and focus instead on trivial items of interest
with impunity// they gloss over the structural racism and
deprivation in our society /and are bereft of any integrity /
and now nothing else is left//
right?

While all this is going on the focus is being diverted / from
the important issues of the day to something more
perverted// if you can't see the dangers of this and the way
it's being applied / then you need to wake up and smell the
coffee 'cos something inside you has died//
so go

# Damn the Virus

Damn the virus
and damn its origins
Damn the spread
that caused the shut ins

Damn the outbreaks
damn the fear
damn those who listened
but refused to hear

Damn the virus
and damn the infection
Damn the extent
of its transmission

Hearts go out to lives
the havoc has wrecked
Damn the cause of this virus
and damn its effects

Damn it now
and damn it tomorrow
Damn it for causing
incredible sorrow

May it return not
now or ever
Damn this virus to hell
and damn it forever

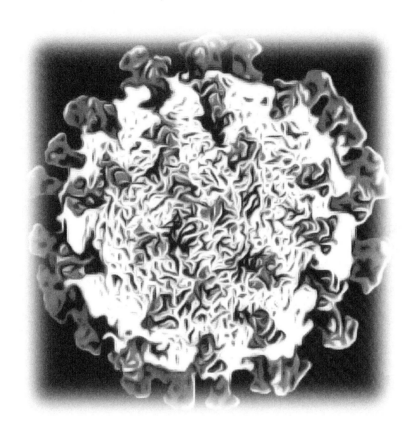

# Gratitude

When it comes to being honest
I can celebrate the fact
That in all my years on this good earth
There is nothing I have lacked

And yet in other countries
People far less fortunate than I
Are forced to live in squalor
And are sick and often die

When it comes to being grateful
I can hold my hand on heart
And hope in others' suffering
I may never play a part

# Boats were sailing

Boats were sailing, sun was shining
People laughing, families dining
Lovers walking, silver lining…
And then the virus came

Jetting off into the sun
Holiday youths having fun
Life for many just begun…
And then the virus came

Weddings organised for Spring
Choosing songs and
hymns to sing
The gifts
excited guests would bring…
And then the virus came

We were singing, we were smiling
Life was good and so beguiling
Now there is no once-in-a-whiling
Since the virus came

# Seaside Poem

Oh I do like to be beside the seaside
with the oil slicks a-washing on the shore
Oh I do like to walk along the promenade
while my feet dodge the hypodermics
and the tar

Oh I do like the sickly smell of ozone
and the sewerage that washes over me
There is nothing to compare
with breathing in polluted air
beside the seaside
beside the sea

# *That

Trying to catch *that thought
*that fleeting phrase that
just this very moment
drifted past me
wanting to breathe in the thin air
but daring not
to even move in case it
dissipates and boils away
vapouring into nothing

But it's vital
that I try to bring into captivity
*that moment,
the emotion that was felt
within a clever wordplay,
laced with humour,
embellished with
simile and alliteration

And while my entire
focus of attention
was on the taming of
*that gossamer glimpse of glory
by the touchstone of a literary phrase
of a perfectly rhythmic composition
everything was ruined when
my clumsy fingers,
the lack of space on

my smartphone touchscreen
and a jaded and cynical
spellchecker tool
conspired together
to spell the crucial word as 'tgat'

● ● ●

# Another circuit of the sun

This week I marked
another circuit of the sun
Another year gone by,
a new one just begun
but this year happy birthday
wasn't sung
because a pandemic
tied our tongues

I spent my birthday
with my closest kin
Marking the day quietly
during the lock in
This year there will be no
night out on the town
Instead an early night
and dressing gown

Tell me, how can I celebrate
when optimism dissipates
and this viral curse accelerates?

While governments anticipate
steep rises in infection rates
with people's livelihoods at stake
not one of us can take a break
just how much more
misery can we take?

How can I eat

another slice of cake?
instead my happiness is fake
no wonder I'm in such a state
celebrations will have to wait

This year my birthday
is nothing special
just one more date

# Soundings

| | |
|---:|:---|
| conversations | voices rant on |
| hear set | the ears |
| listen ... | ... silent |
| the eyes | they see |
| girl ... a telephone | hello? repeating |
| listen ... | ... silent |
| desperation | ... a rope ends it |
| now hear me | am nowhere |
| silent ... | ... listen |

# If ...

If you can keep your chin up
And put your back to the wheel
With your nose to the grindstone
If you can keep on your toes
While putting your best foot forward
And shoulder the responsibility
When bending over backwards
To face the music
If you can grasp the nettle
With both hands
And turn over a new leaf
While keeping your hand in
And getting your finger out
If you can stand on your own two feet
And pull your socks up
While standing tall
If you can keep your feet
Firmly on the ground
And then show a clean pair of heels
And treat those two positions just the same
If you can stick your neck out
And put your head on the block
While holding your head up high
And keeping your ear to the ground
That would be most impressive

And what is more
You'll be a contortionist
My son

# Meds

Remdesivir
and Dexamethasone
are both difficult to say
but they fit in this poem
They could save your life
and they'll definitely help some
As medicines go
they are both
fairly awesome

# Wish List

I thought long and hard
about beefing up my act
by trying to be streetwise
and removing the tact
I thought about trying out
a drum machine
and dressing in a style
that was moody and mean
I tried to show I had
my finger on the pulse
with a Liverpool accent
but it came out false
I tried to come on stage
like a sex machine
but it didn't work out
'cos my shirt wasn't clean
The working class hero
was another ploy
but it all fell flat
and started to annoy
I wanted my persona
to be witty and wise
but a leopard cannot change his spots
no matter how he tries
I wanted my words
to be smart and incisive
But they came out insincere

and it proved to be divisive
I wanted to appeal
to the nation's youth
When all I really needed
was to tell the truth

● ● ●

# Aftermath

When this fierce battle is done and our ordeal ends / and
there is no more cause to shelter from the threat of infection \
we will finally be free to share embraces with our family and
our friends / and shed between ourselves our pent up love
and affection \

As we emerge uncertain, into that tenuous aftermath / and
look back upon the tragedy and loss our hearts endured \
where we no longer have cause to fear, and our joyful
collective laugh / disguises the worst of times to which our
minds were inured \

What will be forever revised and what will remain the same?
/ How might we measure each and every nuance of the
change? \ Will we as a people be intent on assigning any
blame? / Will we trust each other more as we turn to face the
strange? \

As we emerge from our enforced and global hibernation / and
we begin to pick up pieces of lives the storm has scattered \
and a semblance of normality returns once more to our
ravaged nation. / Perhaps we might treasure values that
previously should have mattered \

# Jab

I had the jab,
got the double jab
It stings like hell
and I walk like a crab
My arm's on fire
Call the fire brigade
I need some ice
or a big Band Aid
The jab felt more
like an upper cut
or a size ten boot
right up the butt
I had the jab,
got the double jab
It hurts like a pig
but I'm very glad

# Writers' Block

I haven't
written anything
not a single line
no elegant rhymes
nothing

My pen has dried
my screen has died
my mind is petrified

I haven't written
a poem for
a long time

But then
neither have
Betjeman,
Wordsworth
or Keats

So why should I be worried?

# Hide your ears and eyes

\\

I dread it when the sun goes down
I dread it when the news comes on

    You can laugh at the newspapers
    The sensationalist red tops

        With their hyperbole
        And hearsay

        And the profit making
        Rabble quenching
        Front-paging
        Centre-staging
        Ever-raging
        Fist clenching
        Issue selling
        Gut wrenching
        Editorials

You can take it or leave it

\\

But you can't argue
With full motion
technicolour TV
images of misery

\\

It's the real thing
We dare you
to take the challenge
Take just one sip
we think you will agree…

\\

Closing captions
Run credits
Play signature tune

<    Fade to grey    >

\\

# We are all lost souls together

We are all lost souls together,
each of us looking for a home,
and I guess we all must wander
as we search for our Shalom.

In the dark we grope for exits
but it's the blind leading the blind
and we look in vain
to find perfect peace
but when we do it's ill-defined
and we fail each time
and then we search for any
alternative solution we can find.

We try altering our consciousness
with opiates and wine,
but each and every time
we do we come crashing down
and we're worse off then
than when we first began.
Some look in dark places
and some change their faces,
while others sell their souls
and still others lose control.

We need a plan.
We need a helping hand.

We are all lost souls together
and my greatest fear ever
is that humanity's time
is running out
but not a single one of us
should be in any doubt
that there is someone
in a higher place
who has the power
to transcend time and space
and who intervened personally,
stepping into our history,
revealing to each of us the mystery
of how He can save humanity
from all of its iniquity
and can put our feet
upon a solid rock
to set us free.

He made the plan.
He is our helping hand.

We are all lost souls together
but if you think
I'm gonna waste my time
arguing the toss,
you need to know that life isn't
negotiable and neither is the cross,

because it was the point
in space–time where
He suffered the greatest loss
to bring you and I to the point
where we are compelled to confess
that we have screwed it all up
and created this mess,
and nothing else in this world
or in the next
is gonna make it any less,
or change the fact that
we are collectively
sending out a signal of distress.

He is the man,
and He is holding out
a helping hand.

# Annotation

Am I just an annotation
in the margin of unspoken?
or simply subtle sibilance
of a metaphor unbroken?

Will I see a good conclusion to the
sentence of my pride?
or reveal an indentation
in my pronoun, modified?
If I spoke in incantations
would my adjectives be lies?

If superlatives were similes
would they fall like rain from skies,
provoking senses endlessly
in liturgy and prayer,
to fall with bangs and crashes
on my onomatopoeia?

If all my world were one large stage
as priests and poets claim,
might my heart's alliteration end
in failure or in fame?

Were I to walk throughout my life
with nothing to connote,
I should rightly end as little more
than a superfluous footnote.

# Hiatus

broken windows and the boarded up facades
gazing blindly at the ragged passers-by
shuffling down the cold and empty boulevards
in search of a where, or when, or why

grey skies darkening a sombre, sullen mood
even the carrion birds have lost their voice today
all across this ruined neighbourhood
we re-enact the same absurd and choice-less play

when taking time is all there is to take
this interlude dispels all sense of hope
suspended animation with no break
in cycles running like some torrid tv trope

this slow disaster of unpreparedness
unfolds black wings, engulfing all in reach
the oppressive fearfulness that spreads
robs us of our vision and our speech

# Covidiots

One day
we'll turn the tide
on Covid
But as hard as we try
to find a vaccine
And win the war
against an enemy unseen
I don't think
we'll ever
find a cure
for stupid

# Insomnia (Part 1)

Midnight
but the sleep won't come

Static
between the channels
on my bedside radio
as in some far-off-place
a DJ tells me
what is on his late night mind

The city never sleeps
they say
Perhaps that's why
it always looks so tired

Red tail lights
draw their progress
through a neon jungle
and the headlights trace
kaleidoscopes upon
my bedroom wall

And the night shift starts

Still the heart
but the mind
fights on
with a hundred thoughts
too many thoughts

encroaching on my memory
transgressing on my sanity
reviving the inanity
appealing to my vanity
and every one
is nagging me
to take it to captivity
so I utter a profanity
for the darkness
to leave me be
and still I crave the sanctity
of sleep ...

... and still the mind fights on

When finally
sleep comes

I am
at last
alone

# Kix

Locked down, no nights out, no kix
Box set binging over on Netflix
TV snacking with a chocolate fix
as my melting clock counts off its tix
Count calories in a box of Weetabix
Drinking slowly through a pack of six
Posting a selfie, counting the clix
Instagramming, scrolling through the pix
of dogs and cats and silly pouting chix
all those needy, posing anorexix
a showcase for the narcissistix
Playing classic tracks by Stevie Nix
singer with a flair for dramatix
Pick up guitar, work out those killer lix
Conjuring up some clever magic trix
Make a blazing fire by rubbing stix
Making nooses from my Lego brix
What more is there in this boring mix?
Locked down, what else can you do for kix?

# Insomnia (Part 2)

Why, Oh why
am I at my most creative
when I should be
trying to get some sleep?

Why can't it keep?

Why is it that
I am plagued
with imagery and ideas
just when I should be
entering the land of Nod?

It's all rather odd

How come the small hours of the morning
are the most fertile time
for me to want to create?

It's far too late

How many poems have I lost tonight
consigned to the oblivion

Of my unconscious mind
simply because
I am either too tired
or too lazy
to capture them
and write them down?

Well,
not this one anyway.

# Foreign Skies

under foreign skies
we all wander
our eyes wide, gazing
searching for landmarks
amid unfamiliar places
trying to remember

we are all foreigners
in this distant land
far from our birthplaces
disconnected from our times
severed from our country

our belongings are scattered
across our histories
strewn in the highways
of our memories and
hanging, caught among
the briar thorns of our regrets

how many times
my father
wandered aimlessly
searching for familiar places
he remembered
while the world
around him changed

# Lies, Damn Lies and Politics

Men seek power
and men seek fame
Where dog eats dog
time and time again

Law makers strive
to impose their will
Ideological thinking
is king of the hill

But if your sole intent
is to perpetuate a lie
Then all your laws
can wither and die

We will throw your statutes
onto the street
Where they can be
trampled under our feet

# Twelve Months

Twelve months have gone
and I've lost the will to play
Twelve months of lockdown
I've been fretting away
My rhythm is in spasm
and my chords have holes
My fingering is messy
like a lawn full of moles
My skills drained away
and my technique is rusted
I sound like a cistern
that has recently been busted
A year of quarantine
is this muso's *bête noire*
when I can't even remember
how to strum my guitar

# I Survived

I survived.

The strewn debris
tells of impact,
destruction and injury.

Still I survived.

I walked away
from the wreckage
and the horror
of this collision
and I survived.

Miraculously,
I escaped the flames
to breathe
the cooler air.

I survived
to fight again
another day.

# On second thoughts…

These are my last blank pages
This is a final chance
to tell the truth

Here is
one last opportunity
to speak out and
let the world know
what I really think

To show how I really feel
and loose the
the genuine emotions
that drive me
and reveal
who I really am.

This is my last chance
to make a difference
one final chance
to make an impact

I will tell it like it is
and I won't use any tact

I will be strong
I will steel myself
for impact

I won't care
how people react
I will simply
point out the facts

On second thoughts…

no…
better not

Someone
may be watching

●  ●  ●

If you enjoyed this book, you may also enjoy reading two other titles by Steve Wheeler published by Wheelsong Books:

Urban Voices – Poems by Steve Wheeler

ISBN: 9-798692-556097

A collection of new poems about city life, contains dark, wry and ironic observations on urban life, identity, crime and poverty.

Sacred – Poems by Steve Wheeler

ISBN: 9-798669-576806

A collection of poems charting the author's journey of faith, and exploring love, hope, failure, fear, poverty and racism.

Both titles are available for purchase in paperback and Kindle formats on Amazon.com

Printed in Great Britain
by Amazon

46223345R00067